RAGGEDY ANN
A THANK YOU, PLEASE, AND I LOVE YOU BOOK

Raggedy Ann

A Thank You, Please, and I Love You Book

By Norah Smaridge

Illustrated by June Goldsborough

GOLDEN PRESS
Western Publishing Company, Inc.
Racine, Wisconsin

GOLDEN®, A GOLDEN BOOK®, and GOLDEN PRESS®
are trademarks of Western Publishing Company, Inc.
No part of this book may be reproduced or copied in
any form without written permission from the publisher.

Twentieth Printing, 1979

ISBN 0-307-10487-7

Ann fluffs up the pillow
 and smooths out the sheet.
Her bed is not lumpy
 or bumpy—
 it's neat.
She tucks in the blanket
 and puts on the spread.
No wonder the pup
 loves to sleep on her bed.

Andy is picking up his toys.
His room will soon be neat.
Ann looks in and smiles and says,
"Why, Andy! What a treat!"
He puts away his shoes and shirt,
    a sweater, and some ties....
When friends come in to play today,
    they won't believe their eyes!

Ann holds her puppy safely—
   gently, but firmly, too.
She doesn't want to hurt him,
   he's so very small and new.
When Andy brings the puppy's food,
   Ann puts him down with care.
He tastes the food and finds it good—
   and soon there's no more there!

Ann sometimes goes on shopping trips.
She likes that very much.
She knows that she may LOOK at things
   but never, never TOUCH.
The things in stores are all for sale;
   they are NOT meant for play—
   so, if she damaged anything,
   poor Ann would have to pay.

People are very happy
  to hear Andy on the phone
  because he always says hello
  in such a friendly tone.
He calls his sister to the room
  if she is far away,
  or takes a message for her
  in a very grown-up way.

Here in the sandbox
    our Andy and Ann
    share all of their playthings
    the best way they can.
(To fight in the sandbox
    they know is not wise—
    unless you like sand
    in your mouth, ears, and eyes!)

Andy likes swinging high himself,
　and that's the reason why
　he pushes Ann so hard that soon
　she's way up in the sky!
But when poor Ann calls, "High enough!"
　and squeals for all she's worth,
　he slows her down again with care
　and brings her safe to earth.

Ann's next in turn to pin the tail,
  but Andy's hesitating.
Ann wishes he would hurry,
  for she's getting tired of waiting!
She stands there very quietly, though,
  because she knows it's true
  that if you wait for others
  they will kindly wait for you.

Ann won't give Andy
    a piece of her candy—
    it's not that she's meaning to tease.
He wants it so badly
    she'd give him some gladly—
    but Andy forgot to say PLEASE.

When Ann comes running in from play,
  she always wipes her feet
  in case her shoes are dirty
  from the playground or the street.
It only takes a little time
  (but she is glad, I'm sure,
  she's not a caterpillar, with
  a DOZEN feet or more!).

Andy takes care to close the door
as softly as a mouse,
for then he knows he won't disturb
the people in the house.
He never, never slams the door
(for Ann just might take fright—
and jump—and drop the chocolate cake
she's baking for tonight!).

"My name is Andy," says Andy to Ann,
    and he shakes her hand like a gentleman.
"My name is Ann," says Ann with a smile,
    and she shakes his hand in a friendly style.
Andy and Ann know each other well.
They're very good friends, as you can tell,
    but now they're practicing what to do
    when they meet someone who is really new!

Somebody spilled the milk today!
Ann quickly wipes it up.
She knows just who that someone was—
  and it was *not* the pup!
A spill is such a messy thing,
  but paper towels are handy,
  and Ann is *always* pleased to do
  a little chore for Andy.

Ann puts her boots on by herself.
(It's puddle-y in the street.)
Sometimes she tumbles over,
    but she gets them on her feet.
Of course, it takes her quite a time
    to fasten up her slicker,
    but when she's had more practice,
    she will be a whole lot quicker!

When Ann and Andy sit at meals,
　　they never reach for food,
　　or sprawl,
　　or stick their elbows out.
They know it would be rude.
They sit up straight
　　and pass the salt
　　as grown-up people do,
　　and, though they like dessert the best,
　　they eat their spinach, too!

Ann wants to read a fairy tale,
but Andy wants a scary tale,
and yet they never disagree
about which story it should be.
They choose in turn;
that way it's fun.
(They read *two* tales instead of one!)

When time has come to go to bed,
Ann never starts to pout,
  or whine,
  or fuss,
  or drag her feet
and wear her family out.
She kisses everyone good-night
  and tells the cat and pup,
"The sooner I go off to bed,
  the sooner I'll be up!"

"I'll give you a bear hug," says Andy to Ann,
  and he hugs her and hugs her as tight as he can.
"I love you," says Ann, getting up on her toes,
  and she gives him a kiss on the tip of his nose.
They are fond of each other, it's easy to see,
  and the reason is simple as simple can be!
They use their good manners wherever they go,
  and this makes them *very* nice people to know!